LIGHTNING BOLT BOOKS™

Hero Military Dogs

Jon M. Fishman

Lerner Publications • Minneapolis

Lerner Publications Company
A division of Lerner Publishing Group, Inc.
241 First Avenue North
Minneapolis, MN 55401 USA

For reading levels and more information, look up this title at www.lernerbooks.com.

Library of Congress Cataloging-in-Publication Data

Names: Fishman, Jon M., author.
Title: Hero military dogs / Jon M. Fishman.
Description: Minneapolis, MN : Lerner Publications Company, 2016. | Series: Lightning bolt books:
   hero dogs | Includes bibliographical references and index. | Audience: Age 5–8. | Audience:
   Grades K–3.
Identifiers: LCCN 2016017099 (print) | LCCN 2016017717 (ebook) | ISBN 9781512425437 (lb : alk.
   paper) | ISBN 9781512431094 (pb : alk. paper) | ISBN 9781512428018 (eb pdf)
Subjects: LCSH: Dogs—War use—United States—Juvenile literature.
Classification: LCC UH100 .F57 2016 (print) | LCC UH100 (ebook) | DDC 355.4/24—dc23

LC record available at https://lccn.loc.gov/2016017099

Manufactured in the United States of America
1-41311-23255-4/21/2016

Table of Contents

Guard Dogs

This military dog and its handler are on guard. They are protecting their base from people who shouldn't be there.

Military dogs are soldiers too!

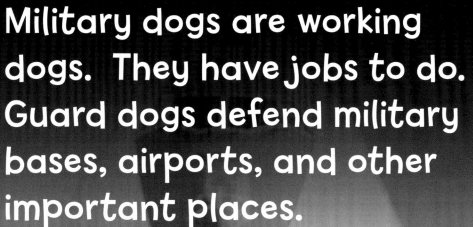

Military dogs are working dogs. They have jobs to do. Guard dogs defend military bases, airports, and other important places.

The United States has hundreds of military bases around the world.

Guard dogs make sure no one sneaks onto military bases. If guard dogs see someone who shouldn't be there, they growl and bark. *Woof, woof!*

Dogs have strong senses of smell and hearing. They may notice things before people do.

When a guard dog starts growling and barking, its handler knows something is wrong. The handler then alerts other soldiers at the base that there is an intruder.

The handler might command a guard dog to bite the intruder. Handlers train military guard dogs to bite on command. The dogs stop biting when the handler tells them to.

This dog is being trained to catch intruders.

Handlers wear bite sleeves to train dogs to bite. The bite sleeve protects the handler.

The main job of guard dogs is to alert handlers. Handlers train guard dogs to bite only as a last resort.

The handler and the guard dog are partners. They train together, and the handler takes care of the dog.

Scout Dogs

Scout dogs and their handlers move quietly. They are on the lookout for traps.

Scout dogs lead the way for military units. The dogs help keep the other soldiers safe.

Scout dogs listen with their large ears. They sniff the ground for signs of enemy soldiers.

A dog's sense of smell is at least one thousand times stronger than a person's.

When a scout dog senses danger, it stops. It faces the danger and freezes. This tells the handler where the trouble is.

Handlers choose dogs to train as military dogs. They start training when the dogs are still puppies.

The puppies must be playful and full of energy. This will make it easier to train them.

Handlers test puppies with toys and games. They want to see which dogs are the most playful.

Detecting Dogs

Handlers train some military dogs to detect bombs. Dogs use their noses to find bombs and other weapons.

Military dogs search
for hidden bombs.
Sometimes bombs are
buried underground.

Detecting dogs
keep soldiers safe!

When a military dog finds a bomb, the dog sits. This alerts the handler that there is a bomb.

Military dogs stay calm when they find a bomb. They don't touch dangerous things.

Other military dogs are trained to find illegal drugs.

It is hard to hide drugs from a dog's powerful nose.

A military dog is trained to find either bombs or drugs. It is never trained to find both. That way, a handler knows right away whether a dog has found drugs or a bomb.

Detecting dogs have to learn different smells. This dog is being tested.

Many detecting dogs go on hundreds of missions. These animals are an important part of keeping everyone safe.

This dog has found something!

Combat Tracker Dogs

Sniff, sniff. This combat tracker dog is on the hunt. It is following a scent.

Combat trackers can follow the scent of things like blood and bombs.

Combat tracker dogs lead other soldiers to enemy hideouts.

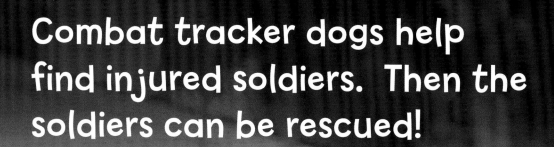

Combat tracker dogs help find injured soldiers. Then the soldiers can be rescued!

This dog is learning to find injured soldiers.

Military dogs may wear special gear. Tough vests protect them from sharp objects.

Doggles protect this dog's eyes. Doggles are goggles for dogs!

Handlers attach cameras to some military dogs. That way, soldiers can see what the dog sees.

Do you see the camera on this dog?

Military dogs live all around the world. They work to keep us safe!

History of Military Dogs

Dogs have been fighting alongside humans for thousands of years.

- There were military dogs in ancient Egypt.

- The Roman Empire put armor on their fighting dogs.

- In 1942, the US military began training dogs. Military dogs played a big role in World War II (1939–1945).

Top Dog

Lucca is a heroic US soldier. The German shepherd mix served in Iraq and Afghanistan. One day in 2012, Lucca detected a bomb. But she was too close. The bomb exploded. Lucca survived but lost one of her front legs that day. She saved the lives of her fellow soldiers.

Lucca still likes to play! She is living with her former handler.

Glossary

base: a place where military forces sleep and keep supplies

bite sleeve: tough fabric that goes over a dog trainer's arm for protection

combat: active fighting in a war

command: a direction to do something

handler: a person who takes care of and commands a military dog

illegal: against the law

intruder: a person who enters a place without permission

mission: a task, or job, that is assigned

Further Reading

Adopt a Retired Military
Working Dog (MWD)
http://www.save-a-vet.org/d7/adopt

Blake, Kevin. *Rescue Dogs.* New York: Bearport,
2016.

The Dogs of the Navy SEALs
http://navyseals.com/2163/the-dogs-of-the
-navy-seals

Military Working Dogs
http://vetsadoptpets.org/militaryworkingdogs
.html

Patent, Dorothy Hinshaw. *Dogs on Duty: Soldiers'
Best Friends on the Battlefield and Beyond.* New
York: Walker, 2012.

Silverman, Buffy. *How Do Tanks Work?* Minneapolis:
Lerner Publications, 2016.

United States War Dog Association
http://www.uswardogs.org

Index

Photo Acknowledgments

The images in this book are used with the permission of: © 501 collection/Alamy, p. 2;
© US Navy/Getty Images, p. 4; US Air Force photo by Josh Plueger, p. 5; US Marine Corps
photo by Cpl. Tyler Giguer, p. 6; © MixPix/Alamy, p. 7; Marine Corps photo by Lance Cpl.
Erick Galera, p. 8; DOD photo by EJ Hersom, p. 9; © US Air Force Photo/Alamy, p. 10; © LUIS
ROBAYO/Stringer/AFP/Getty Images, p. 11; US Army photo by Jason Epperson, p. 12;
© dager/Shutterstock.com, p. 13; © Rita Kochmarjova/Shutterstock.com, p. 14; © Irantzu
Arbaizagoitia/Shutterstock.com, p. 15; © US Marines Photo/Alamy, p. 16; © Everett
Collection Inc/Alamy, p. 17; US Army photo by Gertrud Zach, p. 18; © Pat Canova/Alamy,
p. 19; © iStockphoto.com/slovegrove, p. 20; US Air Force photo by Senior Airman Bahja J.
Jones, p. 21; US Marine Corps photo by Sgt. Tammy K. Hineline, p. 22; US Army photo by Staff
Sgt. Shane Hamann, p. 23; US Navy photo by Mass Communication Specialist Seaman Damian
Berg, p. 24; US Marine Corps photo by Lance Cpl. Austin A. Lewis; p. 25; AP Photo/Freek van
den Bergh/NOVUM POOL, p. 26; JR Ancheta/ZUMAPRESS/Newscom, p. 27; © Gary Friedman/
Contributor/Los Angeles Times/Getty Images, p. 29.

Front cover: US Army photo by Gertrud Zach.

Main body text set in Billy Infant regular 28/36. Typeface provided by SparkType.